POWERING YOUR DESTINY

How to keep a balanced lifestyle; physically, mentally, and spiritually

AUTHOR: GLENDA COKER

TERMS AND CONDITIONS

Note: -The author of this information used the best efforts in preparing this material. The content contained here is for education and informational purposes.

This material is not intended to be a substitute for professional medical advice, diagnosis, or treatment. Always seek the advice of your health care provider with questions you may have about your medical condition.

DISCLAIMER

Powering Your Destiny is a personal reading gift that is given to you only from this publication.

All content including cover design is not to be copied, reproduced, sold, distributed, modified, deviated, transmitted, displayed anywhere including networks, blogs, or websites. Any use of this content and or cover design other than for the reasons stated above is strictly prohibited.

ISBN 978-1-7356677-4-4

TABLE OF CONTENTS

Chapter 1: Nourishing Yourself
Chapter 2: Resting and Sleeping
Chapter 3: Angry Behavior
Chapter 4: Anger Types
Chapter 5: Costs of Anger
Chapter 6: Express Anger! Do Not Hold It In!
Chapter 7: Never Alone
Chapter 8: Kick the Habit
Chapter 9: Strengths and Weaknesses
Chapter 10: Your Spirituality
Chapter 11: Exercising Empowerment
Chapter 12: Change Your Life
13. Conclusion
14. Bible Scriptures
15. Acknowledgments
16. Resources

FOREWARD

Jesus teaches the disciples the Lord's Prayer on the Sermon on the Mount. They are commanded to seek first the kingdom of God and all his righteousness.

Matthew 6:22-23

22. The eye is the lamp of the body. If your eyes are healthy, your   whole body will be full of light.

23. But if your eyes are unhealthy, your whole body will be full of   darkness. If then the light within you is darkness, how great is that darkness! *1.

Daily, we are engaged with the things that matter most to us. We may be so engaged in daily survival; we forget what we need to sustain a balanced life. The important things we put aside are most crucial and are determining factors of how we now survive.

PAY ATTENTION TO YOUR HEALTH

Exercise is the way to go along with eating a high fiber, low-fat diet. You need determination, drive, and the proper mindset to want to be at your overall best. Once you have a healthier lifestyle, you are on your way to making physical moves.

Get rid of any habits that plague your existence. Too much smoking, drinking and drug use of any kind should be eliminated. Drugs may include but not limited to prescriptions, drug store purchases and street illegal. When habits are cut, good health moves in much the same as the shining sun on a lovely, warm day. You will be ready to move to a healthier level.

We must remember to give thanks to our Higher Power for guiding us and giving us our lives. Show thanks and appreciation by stepping up and moving your life forward. Do you want to live a longer, healthier, and happier life? If you seriously want to change your lifestyle and habits, keep on reading. Soon you will be making great strides in accomplishing your desired goals.

CHAPTER 1

NOURISHING YOURSELF

SERVINGS CHART

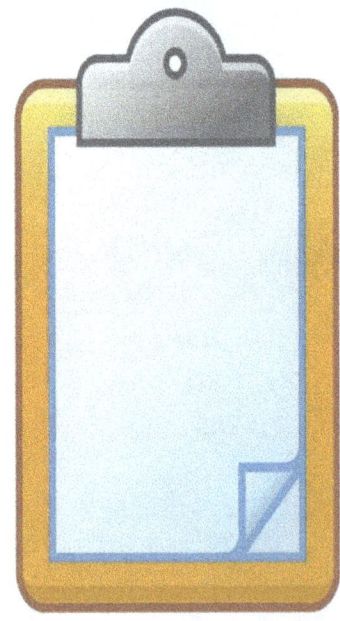

HEALTH FOODS

Foods that contain additives and preservatives contribute to health concerns. Health problems arise when not enough nutrients are ingested. Heart diseases, obesity, and other health conditions surface when high intakes of unhealthy foods are eaten. Focus on eating 3 balanced meals daily.

If you cannot, eat 5 to 6 small portions throughout the day. If you eat this way, it ensures that you are meeting your daily nutritional needs.

Drink 6 to 8 glasses of water a day. Drinking water 30 minutes before and after a meal helps with digestion and curbs cravings.

SERVINGS CHART

Grains: 6 to 8 servings daily

Examples: 1 slice of bread, 1/2 cup of cereal, cooked rice or pasta.

Vegetables: 3 to 5 servings daily

Examples: 1 cup of raw leafy vegetables, 1/2 cup of cooked or raw vegetables.

Fruits: 4 to 5 servings daily

Examples: 1 medium fruit baseball size, 1/2 cup of fruit juice, 1/4 cup of dried fruit.

Dairy products: 2 to 3 servings daily

Examples: 1 cup of milk, 1 cup of yogurt, 1 1/2 ounces of cheese.

Beef, lamb or veal: 3 to 6 ounces cooked daily

Examples: 3 ounces cooked meat (computer mouse size), 3 ounces grilled fish (checkbook size).

Fats and oils: 2 to 3 servings daily

Examples: 1 teaspoon margarine, 1 tablespoon mayonnaise, 1 tablespoon salad dressing.

Nuts, seeds, and legumes: 3 to 4 servings per week

Examples: 2 tablespoons of peanut butter, 1/2 cup of dry beans or peas.

Sweets and added sugars: 0 to 5 servings daily.

Examples: 1 tablespoon of jelly or jam, 1 tablespoon of sugar.

CHAPTER 2

RESTING AND SLEEPING

Z Z Z's

GET SOME REST

It is especially important to allow your body proper rest and sleep. To be refreshed, you must sleep at night and rest when your body needs it. Adults should get an average of 7 to 9 hours of sleep a night. Teenagers need from 8 1/2 to 10 hours a night. During the day if you become tired, rest for 30 minutes.

At work, take your breaks. Do not skip out on them. Keep the room dark when you sleep. Cut off electrical devices. No TV, radio, computer or cell phone. If you must leave your phone on during the night, adjust your ring tone volume to a lower setting. The lesser the distractions, the more assurance of you getting a good night's sleep.

If you are having trouble falling asleep, get up to read a book. Make yourself a soothing drink, such as chamomile tea and before you know it, you will snooze off to sleep. To keep a sound routine for rest and sleep, stay in tune with your body signals.

EXERCISING

Everybody movement you make is exercise. If you stretch, bend, twist, lift an arm or leg, you are burning calories. There are many types of exercises. Aerobics and Pilates are a few. You can walk, jog and bicycle. Join a gym and / or buy your own equipment to work out at home.

Before you exercise, try meditating. It is refreshing and clears your mind of stress. Light a candle or a sweet-smelling incense. Find a quiet spot in your home. You need no distractions. You may prefer to curl up in your favorite chair or sit on the floor, hands in your lap with your legs crossed over each-other. It does not matter as long as you are comfortable and stay focused. If you prefer, listen to soft sounds while meditating. Focus on an object, a joyous moment, or the outcome of your workout.

Meditation is relaxing. It awakens the spiritual mind. Keep your posture straight. Focus and take slow deep breaths until you are relaxed. Exercise is great in reducing stress and increasing energy levels. Try to work out at least 30 minutes a day. If you cannot do 30 minutes, split the time up by doing 15 minutes in the morning and 15 minutes in the afternoon.

While exercising, increase your workout regime by adding weights. Weights tighten muscle mass and increases endurance. Do not force yourself to do any exercise if you have pain. Decrease your workout time or take a break. You will know your limits by listening to your body. Try your best to incorporate exercise daily or a few times a week.

LIFE STRESSORS, STRESS, ANXIETY AND DEPRESSION

STRESS

ANXIETY

DEPRESSION

FACING EMOTIONS

During our lifetime, stress, anxiety and depression are emotions we will face. There is just no getting around it. A part of life is handling problems. Pray to the LORD for deliverance and healing from all ailments. No sincere prayer goes unheard.

Psalm 103:2-5

2. Praise the Lord my soul, and forget not all his benefits:

3. Who forgives all your sins and heals all your diseases,

4. Who redeems your life from the pit and crowns you with love and compassion.

5. Who satisfies your desires with good things so that your youth is renewed like the eagles. *2

Take time to unwind. Practice deep breathing, think and analyze before you move on to an action. When you are calm and take deep breaths, you open your brains endorphin's, which allows you to focus and analyze your problems more. After you've taken time to focus, make your decision and act upon it. Afterwards, let it go. Keep moving. The problem is history.

Know that mistakes will happen. Decisions made may not always give the outcome you expected. Do not fret. Correct the problem the best you can. Do not ponder over it.

Life is way too short to harbor over past disruptions. You must have faith you have done your best. Take any disruptive experience and see it as a learning tool.

Analyze the positives.

- What did you learn from the experience?
- What is it you will or will not do again?
- What can you offer to others who may go through something similar?

Analyze the positives and cross out the negatives. Do not skip these steps. Analyze and take control of your emotions. It opens doors for you to live a more peaceful, happier and healthier life.

CHAPTER 3

ANGRY BEHAVIOR

ANGRY BEHAVIOR

ACTS OF ANGER

Every day, we see angry people. When we do, we want to run the opposite way. No telling when another angry episode may spark, and we don't want to be around any hostility. But what if angry ones live in your home? You cannot escape from them. What if YOU are the main person and have not come to grips to admitting it? What if you are the one causing chaos in the family, upsetting everyone around you?

Too often we seek to blame someone else for our behavior. We don't want to accept we may be the root of the problem. If you find yourself regularly at the center of turmoil, then maybe the ruckus is being caused by YOU. You may or may not know what you are doing. Listen to the surrounding people. If you keep hearing you are the cause, then there may be truths in what you are hearing. Let this be a warning for you to admit YOU are the one causing problems.

Make moves to get your anger under control. This is why you are here. Either you are reading this book to help yourself through anger management issues or seeking to help someone who has anger. Or, you may be here to gain knowledge.

Welcome and thank you for taking time to be here. Use this book as a guide to your everyday living.

If you are the one seeking help, you must first recognize yourself as the problem and be open and willing to change. The faster you are ready, the quicker you will heal. Make a quick observance of others reactions towards you.

Are others nice to you? Do they appear friendly towards you? If they appear standoffish, there may be a reason. You might appear as an angry person to them. Your tone may be harsh and you may not smile much if any. Hard work, prayer and dedication makes changes. Soon, you will live the life you so well deserve.

QUESTIONS TO ASK YOURSELF

- Are you angry most of the time?

- Are you angry to the point you have a facial blood rush?

- Does your blood pressure rise?

- Do you want to hit someone or something?

- How long does your anger bouts last?

- If you get angry at work, do you come home and take it out on the entire family at the dinner table?

- Do you get mad at the least little thing someone says or does to you?

- If someone jumps in front of you in line at the grocery store, does it anger you to the point you want to strike out to hit the person?

- Do you keep your guards up when talking with others?

- Do you search for faults in a conversation when talking to others?

MORE QUESTIONS

- Do you find yourself defensive?

- Do you let anger control your life?

- Do you miss out on family time because you're still angry with what happened to you earlier at school or work?

- Do you have a hard time concentrating on your job or with studies?

- Do you use your anger as a crutch to help you get through life?

- Does a "I'm better than him" attitude make you happy?

- Do you do your best to show out or belittle someone because they   are having problems doing the same task?

- Is your anger intensive or raging?

- Are you able to calm yourself when you are angry?

- Can anyone else calm you when you are angry?

- Do you throw things when angry?

- Do you strike people physically or verbally out of anger?

People with anger issues may feel they are being criticized by others, which makes them defensive. If someone tells you your car lights are on in the store parking lot, you may become angry and defensive when the person is just trying to be helpful.

If the answer is yes to one or more questions, anger management problems exists.

ANGER WARNING SIGNS

WARNING

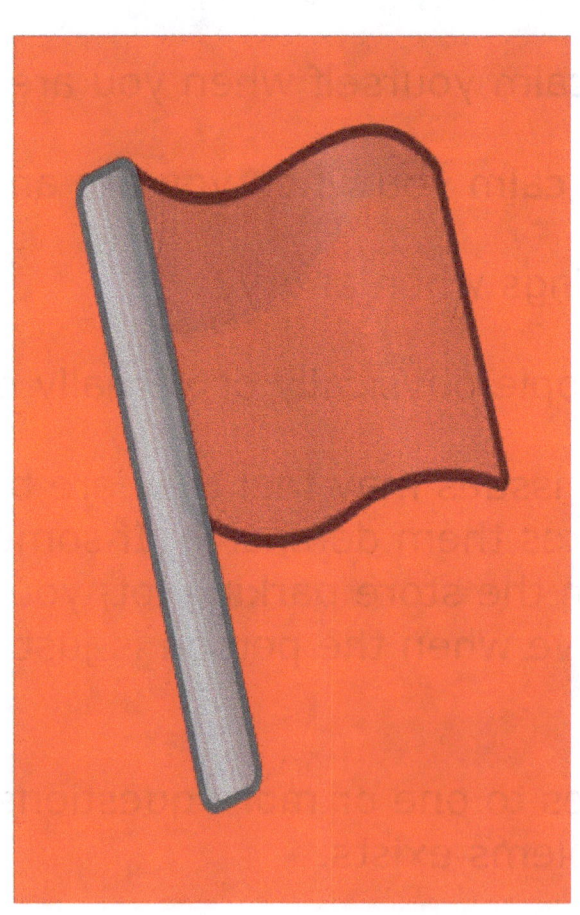

If you are reading this chapter for yourself, you may realize you have a problem with anger management skills. It is good to foresee a problem and face it right away. Here are early warning signs of anger.

PHYSICAL SIGNS OF ESCALATING ANGER:

- Clenching your jaws
- Dizziness
- Grinding your teeth
- Headache
- Rapid heart rate
- Shaking
- Sweating
- Trembling
- Upset stomach

EMOTIONAL ANGER SIGNS:

- You are anxious.
- You are depressed.
- You have feelings of guilt.
- You are irritated.
- You are resentful.
- You are sad.
- You want to strike out, physically or verbally
- You want to run away

TELL-TALE SIGNS:

- Abusive behavior
- Frequent crying
- Pacing the floor
- Pounding your hand with your fist

- Raising your voice

- Rubbing your temples

- Sarcasm Yelling

These are warning signs that anger is getting out of control. If you have a problem causing you to get angry and you notice yourself experiencing a few of these warning signs, try your best to calm yourself.

CHAPTER 4

ANGER TYPES

11 TYPES OF ANGER

There are different things that make us angry for different reasons. To control anger, you need to recognize what you are experiencing. Let's examine more on anger.

BEHAVIORAL ANGER

People who experience behavioral anger will confront the person whom they have issues with. They may be rude to them followed by violent acts.

CHRONIC ANGER

Chronic anger sufferers do not care for anyone. They are clueless why they don't even like themselves. They are angry at the world most times.

CONSTRUCTIVE ANGER

Through anger management techniques, anger is channeled in this way to get the results they seek.

DELIBERATE ANGER

This anger is geared towards people seen as subordinate. The aggressor assumes others are beneath them and may disrespect them. This behavior is usually geared towards a child or someone the aggressor is helping financially or otherwise.

JUDGMENTAL ANGER

This person has low self-esteem issues. They enjoy embarrassing people in public places.

OVERWHELMING ANGER

These people are a snowball of fire. They are angry with themselves and everyone else. The results are physical violence and destruction. They will cause physical harm even to themselves.

PARANOID ANGER

The person is paranoid and is sure someone is against him / her or poking fun. This person will lash out to whom they conceive is their culprit.

PASSIVE ANGER

These people are sarcastic and use mockery to express anger. They have a need to take part in conflict and confrontational scenes, but they shun from it. They see themselves as cowards. This makes them even angrier at themselves. They want to partake but cannot bring themselves to do it.

RETALIATORY ANGER

This one is likely the most common. It occurs as a direct response to someone acting out and causing a disturbance.

SELF-INFLICTED ANGER

People may overeat, starve themselves, or cut themselves. Anger is geared towards punishing others or themselves.

VOLATILE ANGER

This anger is explosive. It comes and goes without warning. It is startling to be around this person because you never know when an outburst of anger is coming, and they may be violent.

Do you identify with any of these acts of anger? What made you angry yesterday, may not make you angry tomorrow. But, be mindful of anger and understand how to best handle each of these in any confrontation that arises.

Psalm 37:8

Refrain from anger and turn from wrath; do not fret – it leads only to evil.

*3

CHAPTER 5

COSTS OF ANGER

COSTS OF ANGER

In life, you pay a high cost just from being angry. Take a look at the below costs. Decide if acting out in anger is worth the damage you are doing to yourself and others.

HEALTH

Chronic high levels of anger wreak havoc on your health. If you often get angry, you are increasing your stress levels. Your heart beats faster and blood pressure levels rise. Anger attacks repeated over time break the body's defenses and cause disastrous effects on your overall health.

RELATIONSHIPS

Frequent anger outbursts destroy families and relationships sometimes to the point of no repair. After you've conquered your anger issues, acquaintances may not be willing to make amends. Pray for the LORD to intervene and love them from a-far, until they accept the new and improved you.

SAFETY

Road rage is a big thing. It's an epidemic these days. So many people drive in anger. They don't care for the lives of others or themselves. Being behind the wheel of a 3,000 or plus pound of steel and fiber is no joke. It can be very dangerous. If you drive in anger, it impairs your judgment, makes you an unsafe driver to yourself, passengers and with whom you share the road.

SELF-ESTEEM

After a verbal battle, you will notice expressing anger often leads to feelings of embarrassment, guilt, remorse, and shame. You realize your reactions are overblown. This causes damage to your self-esteem.

TIME

Little children get angry over small things. They get frustrated because they have trouble expressing what they want. With the proper training, children learn how to express themselves without exerting so much forceful anger. Anger steals away precious moments. Fits of rage robs you from living the true joys of life.

WORKPLACE

Work quality is affected when you are angry. You are not at your best. Your judgment is off, causing you to make poor choices, which could cause you your job. Uncontrollable anger has cost lots of people their jobs.

YOUR CHILDREN

Constant anger can devastate a child, sometimes more so than the experience of a parents' divorce. Until you see the effects of what you are doing through the child's eyes, you may never recognize the true extent of the damage done.

Children first learn behaviors from their parents and act upon them with their siblings and peers. Proper training and teaching comes from the home first, not school. A child should be trained before they go to school. Remember, children often practice and mimic what they see and hear at home.

THE AFTER EFFECTS OF ANGER

Domestic violence is one of the most insidious forms of violence. Anger is a direct cause of this crime. Men commit 95 percent of reported domestic violence.

Domestic violence is the number one reason so many women seek shelters and need emergency medical help. Poor parenting skills coupled with anger lead to the abuse of more and more deaths and injuries among children.

Children who are abused or have seen long time abuse growing up, usually become parents who abuse their own children. It is a cycle coupled with anger and low self-confidence. The person sees him or herself as worthless and out of control. They believe the world is against them and no one cares. Hopelessness sets in and anger escalates to the point of abuse and violence.

In the family, anger rages when the one committing it realizes there will not be any real consequences for their actions. Others in the household see this behavior and act out. Everyone is in a rage. The children who grow up in abusive households learn to act this way. They think is okay to kick, destroy, scream and throw things.

Once the entire family is caught up in this cycle, it's hard to make a change. Family intervention is the only way to get the family back to civilization. When a heated argument or fight is over, reality surfaces. The ones involved come to realize nothing is accomplished by the rage. One good thing is that the cycle of rage can be broken, and peace restored.

CHAPTER 6

EXPRESS ANGER!

DO NOT HOLD IT IN!

Instead of cursing, screaming, throwing things, stomping and hurting those around you, find healthier ways to express anger. In this book, you will learn how to get your anger under control. Your life will be better when you learn how to control your emotions.

No need to go through your life tipping through the daisies wearing rose colored glasses to control anger. I mean, you don't have to become a doormat because you are managing your anger. Anger is a human emotion. It is OK to get angry, but not where it is hard to control yourself. You will learn more productive ways to express anger when it occurs.

HOW TO CONTROL YOUR ANGER

MANAGEMENT TECHNIQUES

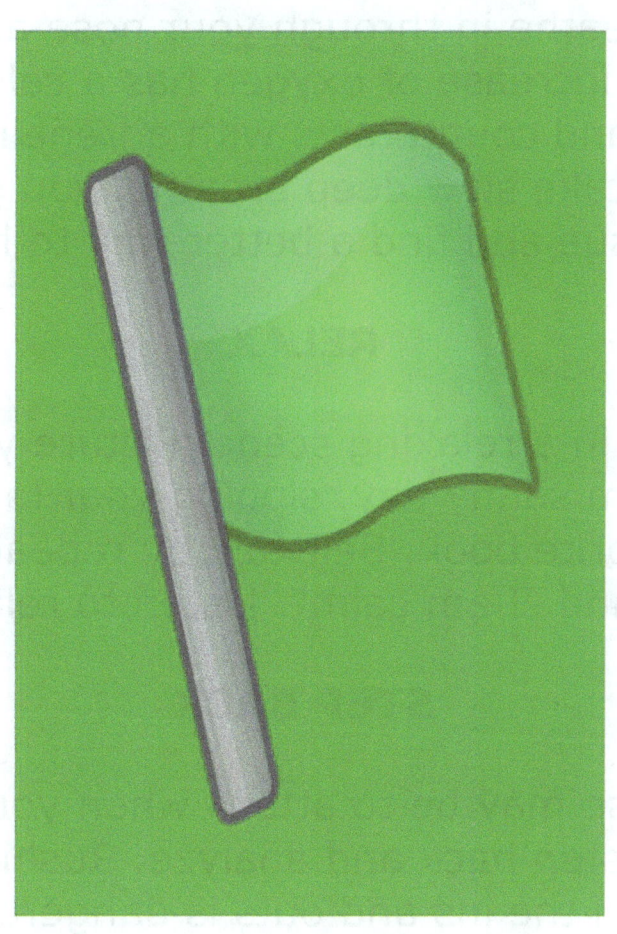

SLOW DOWN AND BREATHE

When people are angry, sometimes they may speak and drive faster. When the pace is picked up due to anger, you are not calm. Try to force yourself to do things slower. Take a few slow deep breaths. Breathe in through your nose and exhale through your mouth. The increase of oxygen has a calming effect on the nervous system and counteracts with adrenaline to make you calm. When you take slow deep breaths, you give yourself time to analyze the issue and find a better way to handle things.

RELAX

Imagine yourself in a relaxing scene. Picture yourself relaxing outside on a warm sunny day, sipping your favorite drink and reading your favorite book. Self-talk by repeating phrases such as "Slow down" and "I am calm". Listen to relaxing music.

STEP BACK

Your first response may be to attack when you are angry. The best choice is to step back and analyze. Rushing into a problem you don't know all the ins and outs is dangerous. Let the other person have their say. Try to understand their point of view. Do not argue with them. Communication is the key and opens the door to understanding.

TAKE A BREAK

Sometimes, you need to do more than trying to talk out an issue. If arguing occurs, stress may be the ignition fuse. Everyone is angry and confused. If the argument is at the point where no one is thinking, it may be best for everyone involved to go their separate ways to cool off. Give it a few minutes, find a time to meet back up or just squash it altogether.

TAKE A WALK

Walk for a few minutes to work off steam and rid frustrations. Walk the dog. Stroll the neighborhood or go to the park to stretch your legs. Any exercise is a stress reliever and gets rid of any anger issues. It even helps to redirect your thoughts.

In the beginning stages of anger, exercise. For a great way to rid stress, exercise regularly. Walk daily or a few times a week. You will notice your anger bouts getting fewer and fewer. When walking, pace yourself. Frantic and rapid walking feeds the anger if you are still brooding. Once you dissipate anger, you will find solutions to your problem.

THINK BEFOREHAND

During the heat of the moment, it might be difficult to stop and think before saying something hurtful. Leave if the bickering escalates. It is better to write what you want to say beforehand if you know you are facing a disagreeable issue. It will help you keep your cool and avoid saying extra things out of the way.

WATCH AN INSTANT REPLAY

When feelings of anger surface, try looking at what is getting you there. Did you hear talk you disagree with? Is it a past problem you remember because of a similar facing problem?

Give yourself time to figure things out and their reasons. After you know what is getting you upset, it will be easier for you to come up with a solution. Replay the scenario in your mind to understand it better. Once you pinpoint the root of what's going on, you can cut the problem entirely.

LISTEN AND LEARN

Listen to what the other person has to say before you get mad. Many people SAY they are listening, but they are just staying quiet temporarily while the other person is speaking. They are plotting out what they will say when they speak . There is a reason we are born with two ears and one mouth. We should listen twice as much as we speak.

We should listen to what the other person is saying, even if they are speaking in anger. Be sure to understand their viewpoint. If you do not, ask them to clarify a point for you, but don't get into a scrambling match.
It makes no sense to get angry or violent.

WALK A MILE IN THEIR SHOES

The next time you get angry because your child did not make his bed the right way, put yourself in his place. He is much shorter than you and cannot make perfect hospital corners. Did your husband forget to pick up juice on his way home from work? Walk a mile in his shoes and see if you can remember to stop at the market after the day he most likely had. If nothing else, put yourself in someone's shoes to experience the receiving end of the anger you're giving out to others.

TALK TO A FRIEND

Call a friend on the phone or send out a text. Go out for lunch or coffee. Just getting out and venting is enough to help you dispel feelings of anger. Be willing to listen to your friends too if they are having issues. It helps them and gives you a new perspective on your problems. By listening to their problem, you may realize that your problems are not so terrible. It also helps to write what bothers you. After you write, get rid of your writings and consider the situation finished.

GET A PET

Try getting a puppy, or a kitten, for your home. A pet makes your heart happy, relieves stress, gives you responsibility and companionship. Your anger will decrease because of the new pet you are growing to love.

POSITIVE SELF-TALK

Have you ever been so angry that you talk to yourself and ponder over your thoughts? You wonder what you should have said or done in an

angry bout. This is called Self-Talk. We do it at times, but maybe not to the extent as someone with anger control issues. By changing the way you self-talk, you will be exercising your anger management strategies effectively.

KISS THE GRUDGE GOODBYE

You cannot expect a person to always agree with you. It is unrealistic. At a point, someone will make you angry. Learn to forgive the other person for your sanity and theirs.

SMILE

It may sound stupid, but when anger rages, smile. Try it, right now. Hold your smile for 5 seconds. It is hard to stay angry when you are smiling, even though it is a forced smile. It is even harder for someone to be mad at YOU if you are smiling!

SOLUTION IDENTITY

Never focus on anger. Pray and focus on practicing peace and serenity throughout your day.

Your inner thoughts, the words you speak to yourself have a great impact on you. If mental self-talk is unfriendly, probable anger will increase. If the mental battle continues, you end up losing. Change your self-talk into something more calming and soothing. Instead of thoughts of, "If he says one more thing, I will explode!", try thinking, "I will take a deep breath, stay calm and get through this".

CHAPTER 7

NEVER ALONE

YOU ARE NEVER ALONE

It is important that you know you are not alone. Everyone experiences anger. The point of learning to manage your anger is not to do away with it. You must learn to channel it in a positive way so you can improve your relationships and way of living.

Uncontrollable rage and anger cause negative effects on your life, but managed anger can change your life to be better. Anger can turn into motivation. Just think for a minute. When you are angry with someone or something at school or work, you work harder. You become angry at yourself for not being able to carry out the task or meet a goal.

Anger turns out to be constructive. If used right, it can be helpful. Anger can help us out of a dangerous issue. For instance, you notice a child run towards the street to get a ball. A car is coming full speed. Your anger at the driver of the car and increased anxiety level causes you to spring into action to save the child. Our body is equipped with reaction signals enabling us to respond quickly to emergencies. In God's image, we are beautifully made.

Genesis 1:26

Then God said, "Let us make mankind in our image, in our likeness, so that they may rule over the fish in the sea and the birds in the sky, over
the livestock and all the wild animals, and over all the creatures that
move along the ground." *4

SUPPORT

Persons may have difficulty admitting a problem. Others may admit it and agree to getting help. There is a great difference in wanting help and receiving it. One may find it a huge task in learning to control anger. Help is needed. A person with anger management issues may be committed to making a change but need a push to take the first steps. The person needs to assure themselves that they are not alone with their problems.

Often they need the help and support of a group. They need support and encouragement to fight their anger control issues. You may talk to your church leader, Christian support group or take an anger management course.

In group settings, there are plenty of people experiencing the same problems. Courses may take a full day and sometimes they may be weekend retreats. Throughout these courses, you are taught useful techniques to manage anger. You learn how to combat frustrations, emotions and discover the triggers for your outbursts. There are many lessons to learn when attending a group setting.

These courses are not just for adults. There are programs for adolescents, children, and teens. The courses for younger people are interesting and age suitable. The activities will teach the young valuable life lessons on emotions as well. Courses are taken with other children experiencing the same issues. Everyone receives lots of encouragement and support.

Whichever way you go, help and support is available. It is overwhelming if you try to conquer your issues alone. Note that members of your family are not equipped with the knowledge and training to help you.

While receiving counseling, you realize people care and are there for you. They want to see you succeed. Get in touch with your church and professional care provider. Do an internet search to find anger management services and check out your local health organizations.

Be prepared when looking for support by knowing your triggers. Keep notes of the things that set off your anger. Whoever you work with will ask questions on your behavior. Prepare notes beforehand to save time. Notes help the professional find the causes of your outbursts and aids in determining the reason you get angry. You are helping the professional make a suitable plan for you.

PHYSICAL SIGNS

As your anger is rising, keep a list of the signs you notice happening, physically and emotionally. Do you get nauseous or sweat right before you get angry? Do you want to scream? Make a note of every happening.

When you find a professional you want to work with, this information will help them to help you that much quicker. For you and the mental health of your family, you can break the cycle. For useful results, do not wait to get the help you need. Start seeking resources right away. It is the best thing you can do for yourself.

Congratulations to you! You are now on your way to living the life you deserve. No longer will anger stand in your way. You can control it and use it in positive ways. If after reading this book, you continue having problems controlling anger, seek professional help. The root of your anger may stem from a deeper psychological standpoint not written in this book. If so, consult a professional. Remember, you do not have to handle your problems alone. God is always near. Call on HIM. You are never alone.

CHAPTER 8

KICK THE HABIT

KICK THE HABIT

Ask yourself if there are any personal habits in your life you want to change. If so, be determined to change. You may need to give up smoking, abusing drugs and other habits that make you seem lost. You may gamble, eat excessively or engage in other habits not mentioned. To be successful at reaching your goal, face the problems right away. Seek the help of a professional. Family and friends may support you in non-professional ways.

Once you decide what you need to improve, make a step-by-step plan. It will take time to get better. Temptations will try to hold you back. Remember, your support team is there for you to help ease your burdens. If family is not there for personal reasons, seek a professional or someone special in your life, past or present.

It may upset and frustrate you to kick a long-term habit. As long as someone is there to help you through the rough times, you will overcome your frustrations. Remember to be honest from the heart. Use support but learn to trust yourself. Take steps in gaining independence. This will boost your self-confidence and make you happier. Remember to show your appreciation to those who are helping you along the way.

INFLUENCES

There are factors that influence the life you live. These influences are natural parts of your life. Together, these parts make you whole. God has equipped our minds to have free will. The steps you take, the choices you make will set the outcome of your life.

Your family, culture and worship are life influences. You may make choices due to how you are raised from childhood and what your religious practices are. This may be your staple of guidelines in how you make life decisions. Your daily associations will affect your decisions.

There are members in the family that may be your strongholds. It may be your mother, father, sibling or another family member. You may have a need to be pleasing to them. You do not want to cause harm or upset them in any way. Often, you think on the consequences of a wrongdoing. Thoughts of love one's dance around in your head regularly. Family has a lot to do with your decisions.

Some people do things without first thinking about their next move. They may say, it felt right to make an unconscious decision. Check out every avenue before you make a choice. Do not let your emotions run away with you. They may be strong, leading into a wrong direction, but you must be stronger.

Point yourself in the right directions. Use your brain to check out things before acting. Be careful not to hang with people who don't have your best interests in mind. If your friends are genuine that's good. There may be times when you meet a not so genuine person. Use your instincts. If your vibes are not good ones, it may be better to cut the association altogether.

CHAPTER 9

STRENGTHS AND WEAKNESSES

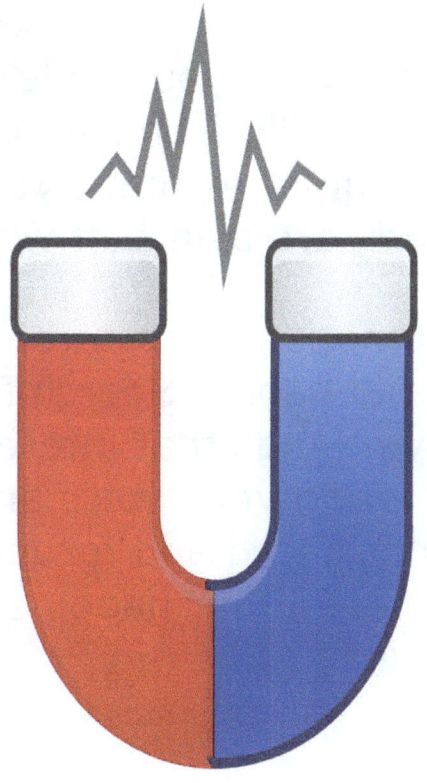

STRENGTHS AND WEAKNESSES

By now, you should be able to see your strengths and weaknesses. Make improvements to strengthen your weaknesses and make your strengths stronger. You will find your challenges allow you the ability to strip the negativity and put on the positive.

Which way will you go? While you are learning and practicing positive ways, there will still be challenges that attack your strengths from time to time. At times you will need a shoulder for support. You already are aware of what to do.

Once you have your emotions in control, start to look for good things to replace the old habits. Search for things that make you happy. Do positive things that interest you. Make sure it surrounds you in achieving your goals and is pleasing in the eyes of God. Stay empowered and focused to make positive moves. Plan steps towards your happiness.

DEALING WITH

EMOTIONS

When dealing with pressures, take time to examine things before reacting. You want to make the best decisions. Get closer to people in your corner. Use them to catch you if you are falling emotionally.

There will be good days and tough one's no matter how hard you try to stay positive. It's just a part of life. Release past pressures. Ease the stress by looking towards the positives right in front of you.

If you need to, talk to a third party. Seek a counselor, clergy, or hire a life coach. Learn how to comfort yourself. You'll see yourself in better light and get extra things off your chest.

CHAPTER 10

YOUR SPIRITUALITY

YOUR SPIRITUALITY

There is strength in the LORD. There are ways to be empowered. Prayer empowers your life. Find your spirituality right inside of you. Give yourself time alone to pray to the Higher Power for guidance and give thanks for your blessings.

Meet with your religious leader who has Scriptural knowledge and advice. You can let go of the weight you carry. Take time for spiritual connections. Gather and seek refuge in the strength of like-minds.

You will find spiritual connections empowering. Learn how to forgive and forget. Let go of negative feelings and look towards the future. Be able to focus on the present. Live your life fully, in a way pleasing to God. Spread His Word. You want no regrets in your life. Show everyone in your life just how much you love them.

Leviticus 19:18

Do not seek revenge or bear a grudge against anyone among your people, but
love your neighbor as yourself. I am the Lord.
*5

**DREAMING
IS BENEFICIAL**

Dreams are powerful and many come true. You will find inspiration when you follow positive dreams. Use your dreams to empower your life and for personal development.

This empowerment comes from inside you mind. Remember your good and bad dreams. Every dream has meaning. Brainstorm emotions and feelings that arise in you after a dream. Dreaming is exhilarating and motivating.

Everyone dreams!

CHAPTER 11

EXERCISING EMPOWERMENT

<<<<<=======POWER =======>>>>>

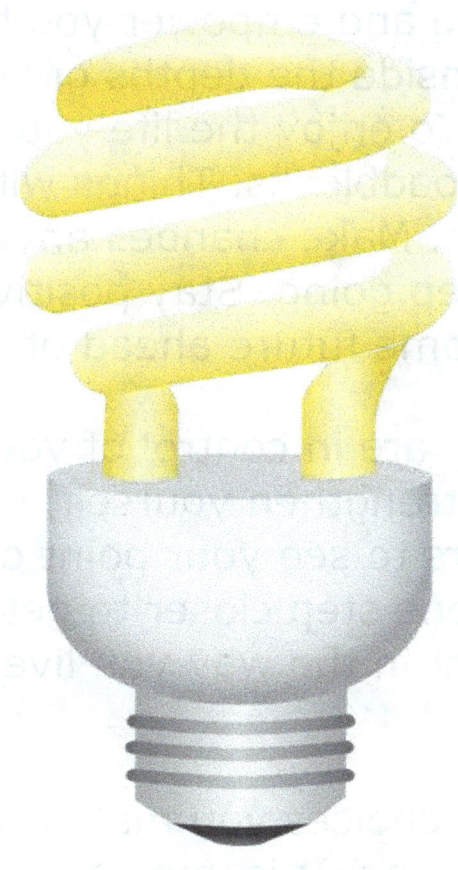

EXERCISING EMPOWERMENT

Most people do not understand how to empower themselves. It takes time to sit and realize what to do to become whole. Figure out what you want in life. Pray and meditate and ask yourself serious questions. What is your purpose on earth? Where are you now in your life? What are your accomplishments? Where do you go from here?

Allow God Almighty to guide and empower you to be the best you can be. Once you dig inside the depths of your mind, begin to make positive changes. To enjoy the life you want, get to work. You will experience roadblocks. Things will not be easy and you will make mistakes. Make changes anyway. Learn from your mistakes and keep going. Stay positive and allow no regrets. You have an awesome future ahead of you.

Happiness begins when you are in control of your life. Once you do what is needed to strengthen yourself, it will be easier to be happier and get others to see your point of view. Empowerment brings you one step closer to getting the things you want in life. Be different in the way you live your life. You are a new person!

Stand to be stronger in the choices you make. Never be afraid to let others hear your opinions. It is important to express your feelings positively. Your self-confidence is boosted, which makes you happier overall.

Are you in an unhealthy relationship? If you are not in a happy and thriving relationship, you need to make changes. This may mean getting out of the relationship. Find someone else or you may prefer to be single. It's up to you which way you go. You may want to stay and work it out. What matters is that you are happy and at peace.

Stand up for what you want. Give yourself a chance to be happy. When you are empowered, you are in control. Use your abilities to direct and enlighten others. People will respect the strong and positive person you have become.

Empowerment increases your ability to make positive choices that produce great outcomes. Empowerment is power. When you have it, you have the ability to be assertive and in authority. These are very strong personality traits.

Empowerment will develop your self-image. When you are using your skills and willing to learn more, you will turn around your life. You're on top of the world. You are better than you've ever been. Praise the Lord!

GOALS PRODUCE

CHANGES

With goals in your life, you have something to look towards. What do you want to achieve? Realize it can become reality. If your goals are overwhelming, there is nothing wrong with changing them to do something obtainable and more realistic.

Nurture your ideas so you can see your success in motion. Goals are so important. Set short and long-term one's so you are always in motion. When you do something that doesn't turn out how you planned, you did not fail. It was a good experience and you learned from it. How you use your goals for personal empowerment is up to you.

In time, you will become smarter and more intelligent for the choices you make. You will see things in a different light and won't even notice negativity lurking because you see positives. You have good habits to display. Once you discover your real chances of success you are changed in every way. The ones who love you and are around you, will notice just how happy you are.

PERSONAL GROWTH

The empowerment you get from personal growth will make you want to reexamine your life's goals. You will forever be in motion, going forward because empowerment makes you move. When you become successful at something you are on the roll to reach out for newer and bigger things. What a changed person you are, inside and out. You see how far you have come. You see the world in a positive light. YOU are in control.

Everything is great!

CHAPTER 12

CHANGE YOUR LIFE

There are ways empowerment changes your life. You need to be positive and open to accept new ideas and opportunities that come your way. You must welcome change, no matter how hard it may be. Change is never easy. Comfort zones are safe and reflecting on the unknown cause anxiety. It is time for new opportunities. The nest must be empty for the bird to fly.

For starters, the mind must open to accept change. Accept yourself for who you are, but do not settle. There is always room for improvement. If you seek more, you will get it with the right mindset. Know the reason change is needed in your life. Write about your life and how you want it to change. In your writings, you will find strength and the motivation to move on to your destination.

If you change your way of thinking, you change your situation.

Life never has to be boring. You have total control over your destiny. What is your destiny? What will you do when you arrive? Once you have the answers, you move closer to your goals and realities. Remember never to stay stagnant. Opportunities are everywhere.

Every time you come closer to reaching your goals, life will become kinder to you. Your life is changing. Your personality is changing. You are open to accepting the goodness life is giving you for the taking.

Change is good. Change is life and life is change. In life, everyone is presented with change. It is best to accept it than not. You do not want to stay stuck in a situation where you are unhappy. In no way is it living a fulfilled life. Everyone deserves to live at their best. You deserve to give yourself the best. It does not matter where you are in life. What matters is where you are headed.

Just by reading this book, you are in action. Your mind is open. You are receiving knowledge and in the beginning stages of reacting to make changes. Change is important towards your life successes. You are in the right mindset. It is time to see your goals come true.

Research is needed to keep progressing. In life, you never stop learning. Find out the pros and cons of your destination. Goals may not be workable at once. Finances may be an issue, but you will find ways to make things happen. When you are empowered, no goal is too far to reach.

Use support for more encouragement. Close family and friends will empower you to stay strong. The changes you are making will be mental and physical ones. You may have to move somewhere else other than where you live to get a fresh start. You may change jobs or become your own boss. Opportunities exist, but you need a plan. When your plan is set, you are on your way to beginning a better life.

When negative things come your way, and they will, remember to keep the positive flowing. Never let the negativity get to you. You will be better not to focus on wrongdoing. Your focus is on things working in your life. You can overcome obstacles by doing positive things. Stay on the positive side. Be aware of the right and wrong things in your life.

If a setback happens, find an alternate plan. When you have a plan for the negatives, you will make positives of it. The best thing to do for yourself is to make the best out of the worst. Let nothing make you unhappy. Let no one make you think your dreams are worthless because they are valuable.

While you are changing your life, things will come your way you will not foresee. Things will happen beyond your expectations. These things will try to push you off your course. Stick to the plan. Once you pull it together, think on what you need to stay there.

Meditate on the consequences of your actions if you begin to stray. Never be afraid to talk with your support team. When you get tempted, reach out. Share with your support your happenings. Lean on them until you can stand up for yourself.

CRITICAL THINKING

Critical thinking is what you are exercising when you empower your mind. This process is where you analyze or reflect on something. Critical thinking is difficult. You need to observe, experiment, reason, and communicate. To see the entire picture and sort through the evidence, for fairness, do external research to learn how the process works.

You will notice it takes work to think critically. You will want to analyze your actions. Are your actions pointing in positive directions? Is what you are doing good for yourself, family and mankind? We do not live on this earth alone. Most times, we depend on each-other for survival. Lights, water, food, and more is needed for survival. Someone had to work today to make it happen.

Step out of the box. You'll gain fresh ideas that no one may have ever thought of. There's always something new and innovative to process. Start and finish your days in prayer, giving all thanks and glory to God Almighty. Help others come to know the Lord and His works. Remember to get plenty of rest at night so that you wake up refreshed and ready to work.

Listen to motivational tapes, read, or watch inspirational movies. As you go throughout your day, give that motivation and inspiration back to others, even if it's just a smile or telling someone, "God bless you." A smile, blessing or simple hello can go a long way in making someone's day brighter.

It brightens your day too! Pray throughout the day, even if it is a mental prayer. Do your best to walk in the ways of the LORD by being a Godly example in everything you do.

CONCLUSION

In conclusion, empower your mindset. You find that by empowering your mind, you will be ready for most anything that comes your way. You are making great choices, taking control of your life and being conscious of what you want.

Remember the good things that make you happy and smile. Know what you are looking for and how to get it. This will be one of the most important things you do for yourself.

Congratulations on becoming a better YOU! Each day, enjoy, embrace and empower living the life you so well deserve!

God bless you!

SCRIPTURES - NIV

*1. Matthew 6:22-23

22. The eye is the lamp of the body. If your eyes are healthy, your whole body will be full of light.

23. But if your eyes are unhealthy, your whole body will be full of darkness. If then the light within you is darkness, how great is that darkness!

*2. Psalm 103:2-5

2. Praise the Lord my soul, and forget not all his benefits:

3. Who forgives all your sins and heals all your diseases,

4. Who redeems your life from the pit and crowns you with love and compassion.

5. Who satisfies your desires with good things so that your youth is renewed like the eagles.

*3. Psalm 37:8

Refrain from anger and turn from wrath; do not fret – it leads only to evil.

*4. Genesis 1:26

Then God said, "Let us make mankind in our image, in our likeness, so that they may rule over the fish in the sea and the birds in the sky, over the livestock and all the wild animals, and over all the creatures that move along the ground."

*5. Leviticus 19:18

Do not seek revenge or bear a grudge against anyone among your people, but love your neighbor as yourself. I am the Lord.

ACKNOWLEDGEMENTS

Special thanks to our Heavenly Father for guiding, inspiring and instructing me throughout life.

Thanks to my family and friends for their devotional love and support.

RESOURCES

www.heart.org www.helpguide.org

Vibrant Life Publishing

HealthonicsHealth

Glenda Coker Network

ABOUT THE AUTHOR

Glenda Coker is from Detroit, Michigan. She is a Christian, inspired writer, Foreign Language English Teacher, Licensed Therapist association and online radio motivator who ministers, intercedes in prayer and prophesizes the Word of God. She is the owner of the Blessings Store at Teespring, which offers T-shirts and accessories. She is the author and editor of four books, which can be found on major book platforms. Through social media, online radio shows and offline affiliations she spreads love to the world, motivating and inspiring people through the Word of God.

"If I can reach just one person, turning his or her life around by shining a positive light through the Word of God, it is a service well done. I aim for more".

Glenda Coker

Blessings Store @ https://teespring.com/stores/blessings-store

Email: glendagrateful@gmail.com

For more information, visit: https://www.linktr.ee/glendacoker

2016

www.ingramcontent.com/pod-product-compliance
Lightning Source LLC
Chambersburg PA
CBHW080442170426
43195CB00017B/2867